Read & Respond

FOR
KS2

Read & Respond

FOR KS2

Author: Chris Lutrario

Editor: Victoria Lee

Assistant Editor: Rachel Mackinnon

Series Designer: Anna Oliwa

Design: Q2A Media

Cover Image: Photonica/Hariet Zucker

Illustrations: George Buchanan

Text © 2007 Chris Lutrario © 2007 Scholastic Ltd

Designed using Adobe InDesign

Published by Scholastic Ltd,
Book End, Range Road, Witney,
Oxfordshire OX29 0YD

www.scholastic.co.uk

Printed by Bell & Bain

89   3 4 5 6

British Library Cataloguing-in-Publication Data
A catalogue record for this book is available from the British Library.
ISBN 0-439-94518-6   ISBN 978-0439-94518-9

Acknowledgements

The publishers gratefully acknowledge permission to reproduce the following copyright material: **George Buchanan** for the re use of illustrations from *Read and Respond: Stig of the Dump* by Angel Scott © 1999, George Buchanan (1999, Scholastic Ltd. **Penguin Group (UK)** for the use of extracts from *Stig of the Dump* by Clive King © 1963, Clive King (1963, Puffin). Every effort has been made to trace copyright holders for the works reproduced in this book, and the publishers apologise for any inadvertent omissions.

Stig of the Dump

About the book

First published in 1963, *Stig of the Dump* is an adventure story in which a young boy, Barney, meets Stig, a survivor or time-traveller from the Stone Age living on the edge of the North Downs. Despite the absence of a shared language, the two become friends. Indeed, Stig is the ideal friend for Barney, the kind of a friend a boy might invent, introducing him to a rougher, less civilised world that releases him from the tidy, nagging order of life at his grandmother's house. As in many stories for children, the main characters are temporarily free from adult control, and thus able to get involved in all kinds of escapades.

Moments of drama and excitement are nicely balanced with moments of humour, much of it stemming from the clash between Stig and Barney's different worlds, especially from Stig's misunderstandings of modern life. Settings, processes (such as making fire) and objects play a large part, and are all fully realised in vivid, detailed descriptions.

The story falls into three parts. First come three introductory chapters. Barney and his sister Lou are staying with their grandmother. Feeling bored and lonely, Barney goes exploring, falls into a chalk-pit and meets Stig. Together they work on Stig's den, making various 'improvements'. Here, the focus is on their developing relationship and the technology of building and furnishing the den.

These chapters are followed by a series of four almost self-contained adventures, which involve a fox hunt, a gang of local boys, two thieves, and an escaped leopard. Lou plays an increasingly important role in some of these adventures.

The final two chapters form a time-shift episode. Barney and Lou are transported back to the Stone Age where they meet Stig and help his tribe move a standing stone into position. Here, the atmosphere becomes more mysterious and evocative.

Stig of the Dump has twice been adapted as a television drama series, in 1981 and 2002. The more recent adaptation departs from the story in several respects, for example, introducing new characters (Barney's grandfather, his mother and her boyfriend) and making more of the Snargets, who feature at the start of the story, chasing Barney into the woods where he meets Stig.

About the author

David Clive King was born in Richmond, Surrey in 1924. When he was two years old, the family moved to a farm on the North Downs – the landscape which forms the setting for *Stig of the Dump*. He was educated at King's School Rochester, Cambridge University and the School of Oriental and African Studies in London. His service with the Royal Navy from 1943–47 took him to many parts of the world. His travels continued as an officer of the British Council. He became a full-time author in 1973. Of his 19 stories for children, *Stig of the Dump*, his third, remains the most popular.

Facts and figures
Stig of the Dump:
First published: 1963
Has sold over a million copies as a Puffin Paperback.
The 2002 television series was filmed around the areas of Darley Dale, Whatstandwell and Alderwasley in Derbyshire.
Clive King's third book.

Chapter 1

Read and review the chapter, which sets the adventure going and introduces the main characters and themes. Focus on the first sentence. Why do the children think the author starts like this? (It makes the reader anticipate this event.) Turning to the meeting between Barney and Stig, ask the children when they first realised that the 'somebody' is Stig. Why does the author postpone telling the reader? (It creates suspense and reflects Barney's own gradual realisation.)

Re-read the description of the chalk-pit (beginning: 'He crawled through…'). What interesting, powerful words does the author use? Invite the children to select a modern object in Stig's den (for example: book, teapot, poker, magazines) and to explain how he uses it.

Ask the children what they have learned about Barney. (He plays by himself; he is truthful.) How do his grandmother and sister react when he tells them what happened? (They do not believe him.)

Chapter 2

This chapter focuses on Barney and Stig's developing relationship and 'technology'. Re-read the passage beginning: 'He *had* fallen, hadn't he?' From whose point of view is the author writing here? (Barney's. Note how the author conveys his thoughts, and track their development.)

How do Barney and Stig communicate? (Through expression and gesture.) What do we learn about Stig? (He is curious and inventive; he is not presented as a barbarian.)

Focusing on the technological content of the chapter, ask the children what Barney and Stig make. (A chimney and a window.) How? (They collaborate, for example, Stig cuts the ends off tins, Barney realises this will make a chimney.)

Chapter 3

This chapter continues to focus on technology and on how Barney and Stig begin to cross the boundary between each other's worlds. Explore the handling of time. What time of year is it now? (Christmas; previously it was autumn.)

Ask the children to describe how Barney and Stig cut down the tree. Point out how they bring the tools and knowledge of their own cultures. Re-read the description of how Stig tries to make fire. How did the children feel when Barney lit a match for Stig? (For example, touched; amused; moved.) Draw together work on this chapter by asking: *How does Barney begin to behave like someone from the Stone Age?* (He goes home carrying a torch and a spear.) *How does Stig begin to behave like a modern man?* (He learns to use matches and a saw.)

Chapter 4

This chapter describes the first real action: the hunt. Ask the children to read up to the point at which Barney says: 'Oh, no, no, no, no, no!' What makes him say this? What does he see Stig doing? (He is hunting the hunters.) Compare this to how he behaves towards the fox. Read the next two paragraphs to confirm that he was aiming an arrow at the horse.

Read on to the end. What is different about the beginning of the second episode? (The narrative focus switches away from Barney and Stig to Lou.) What does Lou see? (A horse with an arrow sticking into its saddle.) Why did Stig shoot at the horse? (He saw it as food.) Prompt the children to compare Stig's view of hunting with the modern one.

Chapter 5

Read and review the whole chapter. Focus first on the Snargets. How does the reader's view of the Snargets change? (At first they are presented as rough and badly behaved; then better qualities, including loyalty and friendliness, are revealed.)

Re-read the passage of dialogue beginning: ' 'Ere, 'oo's chuckin' dirt?' How does the author

Guided reading

show how the Snargets talk? Note how spelling is used to indicate accent (dropped initial 'h' and final 'g') and non-standard dialect features (double negatives). Contrast this with the way Barney speaks, and discuss what can be inferred from this.

Continuing the focus on speech, re-read the conversation between Barney and the Snargets, beginning: 'Cor! It ain't Albert!' Ask the children to identify the many different speech verbs (for example: exclaimed, snapped, piped, sneered) and adverbs (for example: roughly, fiercely, masterfully).

Ask the children what they have learned about Stig, looking especially at his reaction to the youngest Snarget and the jelly-baby. Both suggest his sensitivity, and the latter also indicates his cultural and religious background.

Chapter 6

Read up to the point when Barney says: 'Hey, just a *minute*!' What is he thinking? (The men are thieves after all.) Read on to the end of the chapter.

How can the children tell that the story is set in the past? (For example: Barney has saved 'three shillings and threepence' – explain that this is 'old money'.)

Ask the children what kind of story is being told here. Draw out the idea that this is an adventure, and focus on the features of the genre by asking the children to suggest the most exciting moment and the biggest surprise. How does Stig react when the car falls into the chalk-pit? (He sees it as a hunted animal.) What have the children learned about Barney? (He can act bravely, even recklessly; he is trusting, even gullible.)

Re-read the last paragraph and prompt the children to infer what has happened. (Barney received a reward.) What do different characters know about Stig? (One of the thieves sees 'An 'orrible Fing', but does not know what it is; the grandmother and the policeman do not believe what Barney tells them about Stig.)

Chapter 7

Read the first episode, which sets up the dramatic events that follow. What kind of person is Mrs Fawkham-Greene? How can the children tell? (She is 'posh', as indicated by the way she talks and her 'large shiny car'.) Why does Barney go to Stig? (He wants help.)

A good way to approach the rest of the chapter is to pause at key points for the children to work out what is happening (much of which is only gradually revealed) and to speculate about what might happen. Read the first paragraph of the second part, beginning: 'One or two stars…' What is this passage depicting? (Barney and Lou leaving for the party.) Read on to the sentence: 'Barney thought he knew what *was* going on…' Ask the children to explain what he is thinking. What did Lou see? (Stig, who is following them.) Read to the end and ask the children when they first realised a leopard has escaped from the circus.

Review the whole chapter, looking for more evidence that the story is set in the past. (For example: the circus with its 'Daring Wild Animal Act' would now generally be regarded as cruel; the children dressed as 'cowboys and Indians' – a kind of make-believe popularised by television series of the 1950s and 1960s but a little more unusual today.) Some children might also notice the stereotyped way in which 'rough' boys and 'twittering' girls are presented.

Chapter 8

This chapter introduces the concluding time-shift episode. Read up to the point when Barney and Lou see the camp, stopping at: '…joined in with hand claps and cries.' Ask the children to describe what has happened. (The children have travelled back in time to the Stone Age.) Can the children say when they first realise this? As before, relate the different answers to the planting of clues. Why do the children think the author reveals the time-shift gradually? (It mirrors

Barney and Lou's experience and prompts the reader to speculate.)

Read the next four paragraphs, up to the point when Barney realises that the 'little harpist' is Stig. What is revealed about Stig from this passage? (He is inventive and pioneering in his own time, and something of an outsider.)

Ask the children for suggestions as to how Stig came to be living in the modern world. Read to the end and ask the children what they think will happen next.

Chapter 9

Read the first part (until: '…the tops of the standing stones and…'). Ask questions that prompt speculation about things that are not made explicit. Does Stig recognise Barney? What does Stig say in his speech? Focusing on tone, ask the children if there was anything that made them laugh. (For example: Lou's speech and the offering of food and drink.) Encourage the children to examine how the author accumulates details in the long description of the approach of the stone. What is the climax of this episode? (The moment when Lou rushes under the suspended stone to rescue the baby.) Who prevents the disaster? How? (Barney and Stig, by collaborating, as they have done before.)

Read on to the end. What happens at the episode break? (Barney and Lou return to the modern world.) What remains from the past? (The stones – and Stig.) To round off the reading, ask the children to comment on the ending and to consider questions about the reality of what happens. Did Barney and Lou really go back in time? Where does Stig live? Do the children think he live in both worlds, travelling between them, or just in the modern world? Was Stig real? There is no doubt that Stig is real; many characters see him, not just Barney.

Shared reading

Extract 1

● The first extract, from early in Chapter 1, is one of the many passages in the book where setting and action are depicted in vivid, accurate detail.

● Ask the children to summarise what happens. Explain that the author could have written this episode very briefly. Can the children say what has been added? (A detailed description of the chalk-pit and of Barney's fall into it.)

● Prompt the children to examine how the description is handled. Ask them to identify interesting, precise words (for example: 'looped', 'crumbly', 'rattle'), the names of specific plants, and the use of simile ('like bones'). Highlight these language features in different colours.

● Discuss the effect this has. Draw out the idea that it puts readers 'on the spot', not just 'telling' what happened but 'showing' it. The place is described as if in close-up and Barney's fall is described as if in 'slow motion'.

Extract 2

● Extract 2 is taken from Chapter 5 and describes Barney's approach to the Snargets' shack.

● Read the extract, and ask the children to pinpoint the shift from narrator's voice to character's thoughts. (After the first paragraph.) Mark the text to show how the focus changes back and forth between these voices.

● Ask the children what the reader knows that Barney does not. (The Snargets are luring Barney into a trap.) Note how this is conveyed by switching between Barney's (mistaken) point of view and the authorial voice.

● Encourage the children to find three different ways in which the author reveals Barney's thoughts. (Direct reporting: 'Funny, he thought'; quoting words spoken aloud to himself: 'Pooh! Silly old conkers'; describing: 'He wondered what the valuable thing was'.) Highlight examples.

● Discuss the effect of these 'inside a character's head' techniques. Emphasise that it allows readers to share in a character's thoughts and feelings.

Extract 3

● Extract 3 is part of the long description of the approach of the stone in the final chapter. It is one of several points in the novel where the author gradually reveals what is happening, planting clues and accumulating information that leads up to an eventual realisation.

● After reading the extract, ask the children to identify words and phrases that describe the noise and then the sight. Highlight or underline these. Ask what the children notice.

Draw out the idea that the description of the object becomes increasingly precise and complete as detail is added to detail.

● Now focus attention on Lou and Barney. How do they react to the noise? What do they think it is? Highlight or underline relevant parts of the text. What effect does the description of their reaction have? Note how it puts the reader in the characters' shoes, allowing them to share in the excitement and uncertainty.

Extract 1

He crawled through the rough grass and peered over. The sides of the pit were white chalk, with lines of flints poking out like bones in places. At the top was crumbly brown earth and the roots of the trees that grew on the edge. The roots looped over the edge, twined in the air and grew back into the earth. Some of the trees hung over the edge, holding on desperately by a few roots. The earth and chalk had fallen away beneath them, and one day they too would fall to the bottom of the pit. Strings of ivy and the creeper called Old Man's Beard hung in the air.

Far below was the bottom of the pit. The dump. Barney could see strange bits of wreckage among the moss and elder bushes and nettles. Was that the steering wheel of a ship? The tail of an aeroplane? At least there was a real bicycle. Barney felt sure that he could make it go if only he could get at it. They didn't let him have a bicycle.

Barney wished he was at the bottom of the pit.

And the ground gave way.

Barney felt his head going down and his feet going up. There was a rattle of falling earth beneath him. Then he was falling, still clutching the clump of grass that was falling with him.

'This is what it's like when the ground gives way,' thought Barney. Then he seemed to turn a complete somersault in the air, bumped into a ledge of chalk half-way down, crashed through some creepers and ivy and branches, and landed on a bank of moss.

Illustration © George Buchanan

Extract 2

The Snargets walked off towards the way out of the pit, whistling loudly and banging tins with sticks. Barney waited until he could hear their feet on the lane, dying away.

Funny, he thought. They've gone. Still, perhaps it *is* their dinner time.

He came out from behind his tree and went round the edge of the pit to the low side, and walked along the bottom to the shack the Snargets had built. He wondered what the valuable thing was that  they had left in it. There didn't seem to be anything except a paper bag full of chestnut conkers.

'Pooh! Silly old conkers,' said Barney aloud. 'They're not valuable.'

Perhaps they'd buried something. He dug around in the mossy floor and unearthed a very rusty tin box. It had writing on the outside, he could just make out the letters: 'GOLD BLOCK', it said! It felt heavy. Ought he to open it or not? He decided he would. There was no harm in just looking.

The hinged lid was rusted to the bottom and wouldn't move. He banged at it with a stone. Out fell a rusty mass of screws, nuts, bolts, and curtain rings. Inside the lid of the box was more writing which said that Gold Block was the Finest Pipe Tobacco, Made from Choice Virginia Leaf… Barney threw the tin away in disgust, and a voice said: 'All right mister, come out, we got you covered!'

Illustration © George Buchanan

Extract 3

There was a long time between thumps – Barney counted up to twenty quite slowly, but they kept coming, and they seemed to be coming closer. It could have been the footsteps of some great giant or monster, plodding unhurriedly towards them out of the marshy valley. Barney looked at Lou, and he could see that she was thinking the same thing.

'What can it be, Lou?' he whispered.

'I don't know. Could be anything.'

'Could it be one of those brontosauruses?' but Lou hushed for silence, and then Barney too caught another sound that went with the thumps of the footsteps. Before each thump there was a sort of long-drawn wail, so that it sounded like 'eeeeyoooooooTHUMP… eeeeyooooooTHUMP'… and each time the whole chalky hill shook until they could feel it in their bones, sitting on the springy turf.

Everyone had heard it now, even the chief and the old men, who Barney supposed might be a little deaf. The circle of tribesmen round the fire was breaking up, and everyone was moving towards the edge of the steep slope that plunged down to the valley.

'Come on!' said Barney. 'We've got to see what it is!' They got up and ran with the others.

At the bottom of the valley the forest stretched away to the distant hills under the moonlight, and blankets of low mist lay with the trees poking their heads through them. They strained their eyes to see through the mist where the sounds seemed to be coming from, then Lou gasped and clutched Barney's arm and pointed.

'Look!' she breathed. 'There it is!'

Barney saw it almost at the same moment, though he still didn't know what it was he saw. Out of the mist at the base of the hill, there heaved itself every now and then a dark shape that stood up for a moment and then each time fell forward in their direction.

Plot, character and setting

Stig's den

> **Objective:** To understand how writers create imaginary worlds, evoking them through detail.
> **What you need:** Large sheets of plain paper, copies of *Stig of the Dump*, writing and drawing materials.
> **Cross-curricular links:** Design and technology.

What to do
● Do this activity after the children have read Chapters 1 and 2, much of which is devoted to a detailed description of Stig's den.
● Ask the children to sketch a picture or draw a plan of the den. Prompt them to consider different aspects: its natural setting in the chalk-pit; how Stig has furnished it; how he and Barney 'improved' it, for example, by adding a chimney and window. Explain that they will need to scan the first two chapters for relevant passages and then read closely for significant detail. Explain also that you are not looking for a polished, neat picture but one that shows, accurately and fully, what the den looks like.
● Encourage the children to add explanatory labels, indicating, for example, what things are for, who made them and how.

> **Differentiation**
> **For older/more confident children:** Ask the children to focus on what the den looks like at the end of Chapter 2, when Barney and Stig have worked on it together. This challenges them to consider a longer passage of text.
> **For younger/less confident children:** Suggest that the children focus on just one part of the den at a time, for example, the plumbing system, the chimney or window. They could then produce separate images of these, rather than the whole scene.

Barney and Stig work together

> **Objective:** To identify social and cultural issues in stories.
> **What you need:** Photocopiable page 15, copies of *Stig of the Dump*, writing materials.
> **Cross-curricular links:** Design and technology.

What to do
● The children should attempt this activity when they have read the first three chapters.
● Recall the various technological tasks that Stig and Barney work on. Draw out the idea that they collaborate on these, each bringing the skills and knowledge of their respective times and cultures.
● Hand out copies of the photocopiable sheet, and explain how to use it to explore and record these collaborations.
● Share ideas and prompt the children to relate them to broader themes. How is Stig presented? (Not as an ignorant savage, but as someone who is skilled and inventive.) Does Barney bring civilisation to Stig? (This is debatable. Stig appears to be living successfully and contentedly in the chalk-pit. The things Barney brings – jam jars, tins – can be seen as making Stig's life easier and more comfortable, but does he really need them? Note in particular Stig's reaction to the chimney at the end of Chapter 2.)

> **Differentiation**
> **For older/more confident children:** Encourage the children not just to describe what Stig and Barney *did* but to comment more generally on what this tells us about their cultures and worlds.
> **For younger/less confident children:** Direct the children to the pages they need to re-read to find out about the four tasks on the photocopiable sheet. Ask them to write just one statement, beginning either, 'Barney…' or, 'Stig…', in each 'cell'.

Plot, character and setting

Talking with the Snargets

Objective: To investigate how characters are presented through dialogue.
What you need: Copies of *Stig of the Dump*, writing materials, paper.
Cross-curricular links: Drama.

What to do
● This activity focuses on the long conversation between Barney and the Snargets in Chapter 5, beginning 'Cor! It ain't Albert!' and ending with: 'Run away, will yer?'
● Re-read the beginning of the passage with the class. Identify the first speech verb ('exclaimed') and the first speech adverb ('roughly'). Explain how they indicate how the characters speak and what they are thinking and feeling. Demonstrate reading these bits of dialogue in the tone indicated by these words.
● Organise the children into groups of four and ask them to re-read the conversation, and to find and list as many speech verbs and adverbs as they can.
● Then, ask them to work together to read these lines out loud, taking a part each, omitting the narration. Encourage them to pay special attention to tones of voice and the feeling they express.
● Discuss what readers learn from this conversation about the characters involved.

Differentiation
For older/more confident children: Challenge the children to find all the speech verbs (16 different ones, several repeated) and all the adverbs (nine different, of which 'scornfully' is repeated) and to plan and rehearse a performance of the conversation.
For younger/less confident children: Ask the children to find eight or more verbs and five adverbs. Ask each child in the group to choose a favourite line of dialogue and practise performing it.

What is he like?

Objective: To identify the main characteristics of key characters, drawing on the text to justify views.
What you need: Photocopiable page 16, copies of *Stig of the Dump*, writing materials.

What to do
● As this activity involves taking an overview of Stig and Barney, the children should attempt it after reading the whole novel.
● Ask the children to suggest a few adjectives to describe Barney or Stig. Choose one of the adjectives that has not been included on the photocopiable sheet and ask the children how they know that Stig or Barney has this characteristic. What makes them think he has this quality? Prompt the children refer to the text.
● Hand out the photocopiable sheet, and explain how it is based on the process they have just worked through. The children could work individually, or in pairs, discussing and agreeing on the truth or falsehood of the statements.
● Answers for the first five questions are: False, False, True, False, True. A case could be made either way for the last. The important thing is for the children to find relevant supporting evidence.

Differentiation
For older/more confident children: Encourage the children to go beyond single items of evidence and to consider the characters' typical behaviour, citing examples.
For younger/less confident children: You could provide clues for each statement, directing the children to particular parts of the text, for example, for the fifth question, ask the children to consider what Stig does with the teaspoons. (He uses them to decorate his den.)

Plot, character and setting

Different people, different thoughts

Objective: To discuss characters' feelings, behaviour and relationships.
What you need: Photocopiable page 17, copies of *Stig of the Dump*, writing materials.
Cross-curricular ideas: Citizenship, QCA Unit 02, Choices.

What to do
● Use this activity when the children have read Chapter 6. Much of the fun and drama here comes from the different ways in which different characters respond to the same incident or situation – because they have different perceptions and attitudes.
● Set up the lesson by recalling an incident from another chapter, and ask the children what a character involved in it might have been thinking at that moment. Model how this can be recorded using a thought bubble.

● Hand out copies of the photocopiable sheet. Ask the children to work in pairs: the children can share and develop ideas together, or each can take on the role of one of the characters.
● When they have finished, compare ideas by asking the children to read their suggestions, as if the characters were thinking out loud. Discuss any varying viewpoints asking for reasons.

Differentiation
For older/more confident children: Ask the children to develop each character's thoughts beyond a short, simple statement. They could then go on to discuss why the characters respond as they do, drawing on wider understanding of their preconceptions and attitudes.
For younger/less confident children: Help the children to find the relevant parts of the story, and then to focus on the lines that describe what each character said or did.

Another title

Objective: To understand how chapters are used to collect and order ideas.
What you need: Copies of *Stig of the Dump*, writing materials, paper.

What to do
● The children should try this activity when they have read the whole novel. It gives them an opportunity to identify and consider the major events and themes of each chapter.
● Remind the children of the title of Chapter 6: 'Skinned and Buried'. Ask the children why they think the author chose this title. What does it refer to? (Stig's reaction to the smashed car.) Explain that authors have to make choices when they decide on titles, and that here Clive King could have chosen to focus on some other aspect, for example, the foiled robbery.

● Ask the children to invent new titles for each chapter. Setting this up as a group activity prompts the children to identify possibilities and discuss their merits.
● When they have finished, organise a chapter title quiz. Invite the children to offer a new title; ask the rest of the class to work out which chapter it belongs to. Discuss the effectiveness of alternative titles.

Differentiation
For older/more confident children: Tell the children that all nine titles must be of the same kind, in terms of content (for example, focused on events or characters or themes) or language (for example, all questions or all two words long).
For younger/less confident children: Suggest that all titles focus on Barney and begin with his name, for example, Chapter 1 could be: 'Barney meets Stig'.

Plot, character and setting

Fun and games at the party

Objective: To retell the main points of a story in sequence.
What you need: Photocopiable page 18, copies of *Stig of the Dump*, scissors, glue, writing materials, paper.

What to do
● The children should attempt this activity after reading Chapter 7, 'Party Manners'. The second part of this chapter has a complex, fast-moving plot, rather like that of a farce with its mistaken identities and 'doubles'.
● Hand out the photocopiable sheet and ask the children to complete the activity without looking at the book. Check that they know what to do. First reading the ten statements and then thinking of two more, before cutting and pasting them in order. The decision-making involved means that this works well as a paired or small-group activity

● When they have finished, work through the correct sequence for the ten printed statements: H, D, J, G, E, A, I, F, B, C. You could ask the children to 'mark' their own work. Share additional incidents, and discuss where they fit in the sequence.
● Extend the activity by prompting the children to discuss the qualities of the plot in this chapter.

Differentiation
For older/more confident children: Ask the children to write other additional events on slips of paper and add them to the sequence. Let them create a similar activity for another chapter (but not one of the first three) for other children to try.
For younger/less confident children: If the children have difficulty getting started, tell them which incident comes first. Reduce the number of items to five, and then feed in the others one at a time.

Stepping into the past

Objective: To develop an active attitude towards reading: seeking answers and anticipating events.
What you need: Copies of *Stig of the Dump*, writing materials, paper.

What to do
● The children should attempt this activity when they have finished reading the novel.
● At several points in *Stig of the Dump* the author plants clues for the reader to pick up and reveals a situation gradually. Perhaps the most powerful example of this is the time-shift in Chapter 8. The transformation actually happens when the clock strikes midnight, but it is not entirely evident until much later. This activity enables the children to explore how the author handles this episode in detail.
● Ask the children to re-read part of Chapter

8, starting at: 'They went through the gate...' Invite them to find and list all the clues that suggest Barney and Lou are in the Stone Age. These include the deer, the small size of the chalk-pit, the appearance of the countryside, the absence of buildings, and the camp and the people in it.
● Pool ideas and discuss the effect of describing the time-shift in this way. Ask the children when they first began to think Lou and Barney had gone back in time. When were they sure?

Differentiation
For older/more confident children: Ask the children to read up to the point when Barney recognises Stig and to find at least six details.
For younger/less confident children: Ask the children to focus on a shorter passage, stopping when Barney and Lou see the lights of the camp.

Barney and Stig work together

In Chapters 2 and 3, Barney and Stig work together on the den. Use this chart to record the skills and knowledge that each of them contribute to these four jobs.

	What Stig knows and can do	What Barney knows and can do
Making a chimney.		
Making a window.		
Cutting down a tree and chopping it up.		
Making a fire.		

Illustrations © George Buchanan

What is he like?

Are these statements about Barney and Stig true or false? Circle T or F to give your answer. Then give evidence and reasons for your answer.

Statement	True/False	Evidence and reasons
Barney tells lies.	T F	
Stig is stupid.	T F	
Barney is brave.	T F	
Stig is cruel.	T F	
Stig likes beautiful things.	T F	
Barney is foolish.	T F	

READ & RESPOND: Activities based on *Stig of the Dump*

■ SCHOLASTIC
www.scholastic.co.uk

Different people, different thoughts

In Chapter 6 different characters have different ideas about what is going on. Write down what these characters might be thinking in the thought bubbles.

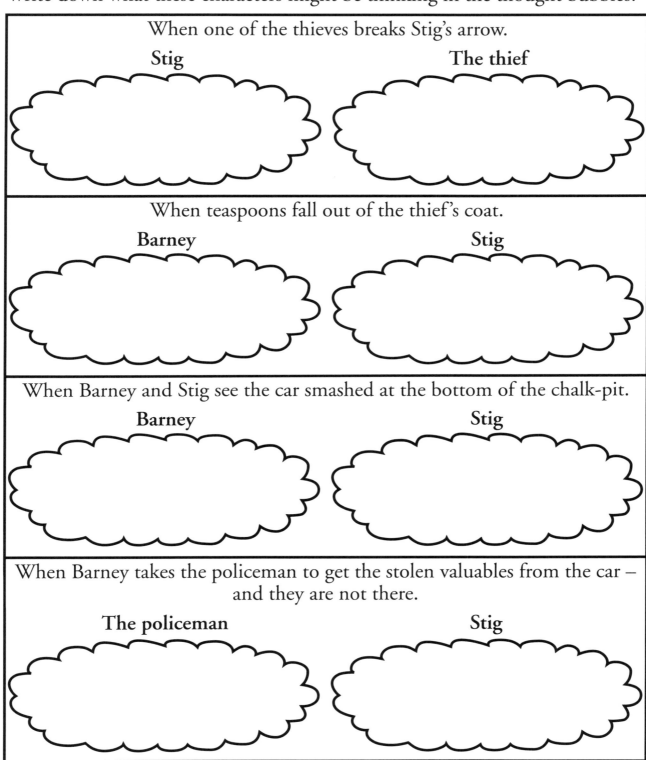

When one of the thieves breaks Stig's arrow.

Stig

The thief

When teaspoons fall out of the thief's coat.

Barney

Stig

When Barney and Stig see the car smashed at the bottom of the chalk-pit.

Barney

Stig

When Barney takes the policeman to get the stolen valuables from the car – and they are not there.

The policeman

Stig

Fun and games at the party

Read the ten statements from chapter 7. Then think of two more things that happen in this chapter, and write them in the two blank boxes. Cut out the statements and put them in the right order.

A Lou organises a leopard hunt.	**B** Mrs Fawkham-Greene tells all the children to come inside.
C A man in a raincoat says a leopard has escaped from the circus.	**D** Barney and Lou hold hands.
E The lights go out.	**F** Barney hits the leopard's tail with his axe.
G Mrs Fawkham-Greene organises a dance.	**H** Lou creeps up behind Barney and jumps out at him.
I Barney and a boy dressed as an Indian see two leopards in the stable yard.	**J** Barney sees Stig hiding in the bushes.

Talk about it

Barney, Gran and Lou

> **Objective:** To invent new scenes for a story.
> **What you need:** Three chairs and a table, copies of *Stig of the Dump*.
> **Cross-curricular links:** Drama.

What to do
● Use this activity when the children have read Chapter 2, 'Digging With Stig'.
● Look again at the end of the first chapter, where Barney gives his grandmother and sister a truthful account of what he has been doing and they react with incredulity or dismiss what he says. Explain that several other chapters will end like this – but not Chapter 2.
● Organise the children into groups of three, with roles as Barney, Lou and Gran. Ask them to improvise the conversation that they might have had when Barney got home that evening. Prompt 'Barney' to begin by recounting something that he did, and the other two to follow up with questions and comments.
● Create a simple 'tea-time' set, and choose groups to present their conversations to the rest of the class.

> **Differentiation**
> **For older/more confident children:** Encourage the children to develop the three roles equally. This involves giving Lou and Gran larger parts than they generally have in the novel.
> **For younger/less confident children:** Structure the activity by giving 'Barney' a simple prompt sheet with brief descriptions of what he and Stig do in this chapter. Ask him to elaborate the first one in role and then pause for 'Lou' and 'Gran' to question and comment before going on to the others.

Stig talks!

> **Objective:** To respond to characters' feelings, behaviour and and relationships.
> **What you need:** Copies of *Stig of the Dump*.
> **Cross-curricular links:** Drama.

What to do
● The children should attempt this activity when they have read up to the end of Chapter 4.
● Re-read a short extract in which Barney and Stig interact but do not communicate in words. Discuss why this is, and ask the children to imagine that Stig can speak modern English.
● Organise the children into pairs, with roles as Barney and Stig. Ask them to choose a moment when they try to communicate, for example, during work at the den in Chapters 2 and 3 or during the hunt in Chapter 4.
● Give them time to discuss and plan a conversation. Focus attention on key questions, for example, how each of them is feeling, or what each wants the other to know or do.
● Choose pairs to present their conversations. Discuss their plausibility. Is this what they might have said? Why? Why not?

> **Differentiation**
> **For older/more confident children:** Encourage the children to develop their conversations into a performance with gesture and action. Group pairs into fours to evaluate each other's work and suggest improvements.
> **For younger/less confident children:** Focus the activity by asking the children to present brief exchanges from Chapter 4: when Barney stops Stig from catching a squirrel; when Barney scatters the pigeons; when Stig shoots a pheasant; when Stig stops Barney from throwing his spear at a fox; when Barney sees Stig aiming an arrow at a horse.

Talk about it

Barney on television

> **Objective:** To create a first-person account of an incident.
> **What you need:** Copies of *Stig of the Dump*, chairs to make a simple television studio set.

What to do
● The children will need to have read Chapter 7, 'Party Manners' before they take part in this activity.
● Organise the children into pairs and ask them to choose one of the more public incidents, for example: the thieves or the escaped leopard. Introduce the scenario: a television news reporter has found out about what happened and has gone to interview Barney. Assign roles as Barney and the reporter. Give the children time to re-read and refresh their memory of events and ask the 'reporter' to prepare questions to ask.

Explain that they will need to decide what the reporter does and does not know.
● Ask the children to improvise the interviews. Choose some pairs to present their interviews using the studio set.
● On a later occasion, the pair could swap roles and improvise an interview about another incident.

> **Differentiation**
> **For older/more confident children:** Encourage the interviewer to listen carefully and to ask follow-up questions. Re-form groups to add a third role: that of news presenter to provide background information and introduce the interview.
> **For younger/less confident children:** Provide a prompt sheet listing the main events of the incident. Suggest that the interviewer ask questions beginning with different question words.

Who is it?

> **Objective:** To identify main and recurring characters.
> **What you need:** Photocopiable page 22, copies of *Stig of the Dump*, scissors.

What to do
● Use this activity once the children have finished the book.
● Organise the class into small groups. Give each group a copy of the photocopiable sheet, cut into 12 cards, arranged upside down in a pile.
● Write on the board the following instructions: Each player chooses one card and reads it without letting the other players see. Players then think of two 'Who is it?' questions. For example 'She's got a posh car, who is it?'. If nobody guesses correctly after the first question, move onto the second. If, again, nobody guesses you win.
● Ask the children to read the instructions and check that they understand how the game works. Explain that, after taking their card, they should give themselves some thinking time to

consider who the character is. Prompt them to consider different aspects, for example: what the characters do; their relationships with other characters; their personalities; objects and places associated with them.
● Draw out the idea that to win the game the children need to think of something about the character that is true but not so obvious as to reveal his or her identity right away.
● Run the game so that each child has a turn. Repeat with the remaining cards.

> **Differentiation**
> **For older/more confident children:** Encourage the children to focus on broader, more subtle aspects of character, for example, presentation and role in the story. Make the game harder to win by increasing the number of clues from two to five.
> **For younger/less confident children:** Play with just a selection of the cards, omitting those for characters with less important roles. Help the children focus their clues, for example, by describing things the character did or said, and choosing describing words.

Talk about it

All about Stig

> **Objective:** To develop an active attitude towards reading: seeking answers and speculating.
> **What you need:** Photocopiable page 23, copies of *Stig of the Dump*, writing materials, scissors.
> **Cross-curricular links:** Citizenship; PSHE.

What to do

● This activity is designed to prompt the children to speculate about the character of Stig and his role in the story, focusing on points that are left open to interpretation.

● Organise the class into small groups, give each a copy of the photocopiable sheet and check that the children understand how the activity works. Make it clear that everyone in the group should get a chance to respond to each statement and that you want them to take their time deciding in which category to place the statements.

● When the children have finished discussing and sorting the statements bring the class back together. Choose one statement and ask one group to say which pile (Agree, Disagree, Not sure) they have assigned it to, and to briefly give their reasons. Ask other groups if they agree; if not, continue the discussion as a class, sharing and refining ideas and trying to reach agreement. Repeat this process with the other statements.

> **Differentiation**
> **For older/more confident children:** Encourage the children to refer to the text to support their ideas. Give someone in the group the role of 'devil's advocate' – to test the consensus view.
> **For younger/less confident children:** Join in the group discussions briefly to prompt the children to respond to each other's comments, modelling strategies for this, for example: 'I agree, and there is another reason too…'

Persuade me!

> **Objective:** To discuss the enduring appeal of a 'classic' text.
> **What you need:** Photocopiable page 24, copies of *Stig of the Dump*, writing materials, paper, television adaptation of *Stig of the Dump* (optional).

What to do

● This is an activity for children to try after reading the novel.

● Set up the scenario on which the activity is based: imagine that a director is trying to persuade a film or television producer (the person with the money) to make a film version of *Stig of the Dump*.

● Organise the class into groups of four, with two in role as directors and two as producers. Give the 'directors' a copy of the photocopiable sheet to help them think about why this story would make a good film. Ask the 'producers' to think of questions to ask the 'directors'. Give the children pens or pencils and paper for making notes.

● After some thinking time, ask the 'directors' to start persuading the 'producers'. Remind them that they need to use powerful, persuasive language. Explain that the 'producers' should listen, question and comment.

● When they have finished, ask the pairs of 'producers' to share and explain their decisions.

● A good way of following up this activity would be for the children to watch part of one of the television adaptations of the novel (copyright permitting).

> **Differentiation**
> **For older/more confident children:** Encourage the children to support their 'pitch' by referring to the detail of the text.
> **For younger/less confident children:** The children could work in a larger group with four directors, each focusing on different aspects of the novel.

Who is it?

Grandmother	The policeman	Lou
Barney	The thieves	Barney and Lou's mother and father
Stig	The Stone Age chief	The youngest Snarget boy
Mrs Fawkham-Greene	The boy at the party dressed as an Indian chief	The man from Bottom's Circus

All about Stig

Cut out these seven statements. Discuss them together and sort them into three piles.

Stig is not real. Barney just imagines him.	Stig is a survivor from the Stone Age.
Stig is a time-traveller. Sometimes he lives in the modern world. Sometimes he lives in the Stone Age.	Stig would make a good odd-job man.
Stig is the perfect friend for Barney.	Stig is the most important character in the story.
Stig does not understand anything about the modern world.	AGREE DISAGREE NOT SURE

Illustration © George Buchanan

Persuade me!

Use this prompt sheet to help you prepare for your meeting with the producers. Think about how to answer each of the questions. Think of powerful ways of making your case. Make notes to help you remember.

Appeal: What is the main reason why this story will make a good film? What is special about it?	**Audience:** Who will the film appeal to? Why? Persuade the producers that LOTS of people will want to see it.
Characters: Who is in the story? What are they like? Why are they appealing and interesting?	**Plot and action:** What happens in the story? Why is it appealing, interesting, exciting? Choose some moments to describe.
Setting: Where does the story take place? Why is this setting appealing and interesting?	**Atmosphere:** How will the film make the audience feel? Excited? Scared? Sad? Amused?

Illustration © George Buchanan

Get writing

That's not what it's for, Stig!

> **Objective:** To write a new scene for a story.
> **What you need:** Copies of *Stig of the Dump*, writing materials, paper.

What to do

● It would be best for the children to attempt this activity while Chapter 5, 'The Snargets', is still fresh in their minds.

● Remind the children of the episode when the Snargets try to make friends with Barney and Stig and offer them jelly-babies, sherbert and cigarettes. Note how Stig misunderstands what these things are for and 'misuses' them in ways that indicate his own cultural perspective.

● Give pairs of children a few minutes to think of three things that the Snargets might offer if the story were set in the present day and what Stig might do with them, for example: stringy cheese; a mobile phone; yogurt in a plastic tube. Share and record ideas. Prompt the children to consider why Stig would 'misuse' them and what this reveals about his world.

● Ask the children to choose three modern objects, drawing on the class list or their own ideas, and write a new episode in which Stig is offered these things and misunderstands their uses. They could try this as either a narrative or a playscript.

> **Differentiation**
> **For older/more confident children:** Encourage the children to write an extended episode involving a sequence of objects. Challenge them to exploit the humorous possibilities of Stig's misunderstandings.
> **For younger/less confident children:** Help the children to structure an episode. (What do the Snargets offer? What does Barney do with it? What does Stig do with it?)

Front-page news

> **Objective:** To change point of view by telling an incident from a different perspective.
> **What you need:** Photocopiable page 28, copies of *Stig of the Dump*, writing materials.
> **Cross-curricular links:** Citizenship, QCA Unit 11, In the media – what's the news?

What to do

● The children should try this activity when they have read the first seven chapters.

● Set the scenario: a newspaper reporter has found out about Barney's involvement in foiling the thieves or recapturing the leopard. The children are to take on the role of this reporter and write a news story about the incident.

● Prompt the children to recall the sequence of events in these episodes and the characters involved.

● Distribute the photocopiable sheet and use this to remind the children of the language and organisational features of journalistic style: the short, attention-grabbing headline; the 'strap line' developing the headline; the lead sentence encapsulating the story. Note also that news stories often include quotations from those involved in the event. Who might be quoted in these news stories? What might they say?

● Ask the children to use the photocopiable sheet to plan and then write a news story about the incident they have chosen.

> **Differentiation**
> **For older/more confident children:** Encourage the children to adopt journalistic style fully, perhaps giving them additional models for this.
> **For younger/less confident children:** Help the children to begin by identifying just a small number of key events to cover in their news stories and suggest that each of these forms a paragraph.

Get writing

With love from Barney

> **Objective:** To write a character's own account of an incident in the first person.
> **What you need:** Copies of *Stig of the Dump*, writing materials, flipchart or board, paper.

What to do
● This activity can be carried out at any time after the children have read about half of the novel.
● Prompt the children to identify 'gaps' in the story. For example, at the end of Chapter 2, it is autumn; at the start of Chapter 3 it is Christmas. Where is Barney during the intervening time? Presumably, he is living with his parents and going to school.
● Ask the children to imagine that in this unreported life Barney has a friend to whom he writes when he is staying with his grandmother and having adventures with Stig. Ask them to write a letter in role as Barney telling this friend about what has been happening.
● Use shared writing strategies to model the letter, in particular to establish that it is in the first person and in a personal style.
● When the children have finished, ask pairs to swap and read the letters. Set up a written dialogue by asking the children to reply in role as Barney's friend.

> **Differentiation**
> **For older/more confident children:** Encourage the children to write not just about what happens but also to convey Barney's thoughts and feelings.
> **For younger/less confident children:** Limit the scale of the task by asking the children to write a postcard about just one event. You could cut out pieces of card to the appropriate size and shape.

Living in the Stone Age

> **Objective:** To identify social and cultural issues in a story.
> **What you need:** Photocopiable page 29, copies of *Stig of the Dump*, writing materials, paper.
> **Cross-curricular links:** History.

What to do
● Use this is activity when the children have finished the novel.
● Ask the children: *Who is Stig?* Establish that he has somehow survived from the Stone Age. Focusing on the last two chapters, tell the children to think of three things they learn about life in the Stone Age. Share just a few ideas, checking against the text.
● Distribute the photocopiable sheet and ask the children to use this to plan a report about life in the Stone Age, drawing on information from the whole story. Emphasise that they should write just brief notes as reminders.
● Afterwards, ask the children to use their notes as the basis for writing an extended report. Encourage them to consider the different forms this might take, for example: a poster; a double-page spread from an information book; a series of linked web pages.
● Remind the children about the features of a non-chronological report, including headings and subheadings.

> **Differentiation**
> **For older/more confident children:** After planning, prompt the children to consider any questions that remain unanswered. Using information sources, ask them to research three questions and to incorporate this material in their report.
> **For younger/less confident children:** Let the children use the headings on the photocopiable sheet and write just one or two facts for each. Alternatively, they could write a list of 'Stunning Stone Age Facts'.

Get writing

A portrait of Barney

Objective: To write a portrait of a character.
What you need: Copies of *Stig of the Dump*, writing materials, flipchart or board, paper.
Cross-curricular links: Art and design.

What to do

● The children need to have read enough of the story to have formed a good understanding of Barney's personality and behaviour.

● In pairs, ask the children to consider what kind of boy Barney is. (For example: brave; trusting; clever.) Share ideas as a class, prompting the children to support their suggestions by referring to what happens in the story.

● Guide the children to think about different issues, for example: Barney's relationships with other people or whether he changes. It would also be interesting to consider what the reader

does *not* learn about Barney, for example: what he looks like, and his home and parents.

● Ask the children to write a portrait of Barney. To support this, you could display a selection of words and phrases for the children to refer to, for example: brave; foolish; change; his grandmother; his happiest moment.

● Share and discuss the children's completed work. What is the most important thing about Barney? Is there anything the children disagree on?

Differentiation
For older/more confident children: Encourage the children to cover a wide range of issues and to consider why Stig is the perfect friend for Barney.
For younger/less confident children: The children could draw a picture of what they think Barney looks like and surround it with sentences describing him.

A meeting across time

Objective: To use reading as a model for writing own stories.
What you need: Photocopiable page 30, writing materials, paper.
Cross-curricular links: History.

What to do

● Use this activity after the children have completed the novel.

● The lesson focuses on the meeting between a character of the present day with a character from the past. Prompt the children to recall how this works in *Stig of the Dump*. (Who meets? How? Where? What do they do? How are they different?)

● Tell the children that you want them to invent a story in which a child living in the present meets someone from the past. Encourage them to choose a period with which they are familiar from work in history. Select one possibility,

and discuss aspects of it they could focus on, for example: a Victorian school pupil or an Elizabethan actor.

● Hand out the photocopiable sheet to each child and briefly explain how this can be used to make decisions about the meeting of these two characters.

● When the children have completed this planning stage, ask them to write an account of the first meeting.

Differentiation
For older/more confident children: Encourage the children to elaborate the episode by including detail and dialogue, and by focusing on underlying issues, especially differences in attitude and understanding.
For younger/less confident children: Suggest that the children work in pairs on the planning sheet and then develop their ideas through role play – one playing 'the character from the present', the other 'the character from the past'.

Front-page news

Use this layout to write a news story about an incident in *Stig of the Dump*.

Headline

Strap line

Lead sentence

Photograph

Paragraph 1

Caption

Paragraph 2

Paragraph 4

Paragraph 3

Paragraph 5

www.scholastic.co.uk

READ & RESPOND: Activities based on *Stig of the Dump*

Living in the Stone Age

Use this chart to plan a report about life in the Stone Age.
Write short notes in each box.

Hunting	Making fire
Food and drink	**Clothing**
Tools and weapons	**Art (drawing and music)**
Rituals and ritual sites	**Anything else?**

Illustration © George Buchanan

A meeting across time

Answer the questions to plan your time-shift story.

Who are your two characters?	
The character from the present:	The character from the past:

Where do they meet?

How do they meet?

How do they react to each other? What do they say? (THINK: *Do they understand what is happening? Do they like each other?)*

How are they different? (THINK: *What happens to show that they are different? What are they wearing? How do they behave?)*

What do they do together?

What do they learn from each other?

READ & RESPOND: Activities based on *Stig of the Dump*

Assessment

Assessment advice

Stig of the Dump is in most ways a straightforward novel. There are no great secrets or enigmas to puzzle out; broader themes and issues are close to the surface. However, the richness of the story means that there is much for the children to make sense of and appreciate. Useful focuses for assessment include the following:

● What happens: the plot is often complex and fast moving, especially in Chapters 6 and 7. Check that the children understand the sequence of events and how they are linked.

● The 'reality status' of the story: ask if the children think the events really happen. In one sense, of course, they could not have: a boy living in the 1960s could not meet a 'caveman'. But Clive King makes it all so real that we believe it. Note how Stig's reality is confirmed because so many people see him.

● The relationship between Stig and Barney: discuss how Stig makes an ideal friend for Barney, someone with whom he can have adventures, build a den and get dirty.

● Genre: Stig of the Dump is at heart an adventure story. Ask the children why they think Barney is able to have these adventures. (Because he is free of adult control.) Note that this is a common device in children's fiction.

Teapots, tins and other things

> **Objective:** To understand the part that objects play in the story, appreciating their significance at different levels.
> **What you need:** Photocopiable page 32, writing materials.

What to do

● *Stig of the Dump* is a very down-to-earth novel, full of objects, processes and places. An illuminating way of assessing the children's understanding is to ask them to explain the role of selected objects in the story.

● Hand out individual copies of the photocopiable sheet, and ask the children to write about when and how the objects feature in the story and why they are important.

● In assessing the children's work, look for responses that go beyond the simplest factual level to indicate appreciation of broader themes and issues.

● Teapot: part of the furnishings of Stig's den, where he makes it into a lamp. Indicates his inventiveness.

● Tins: Barney brings these to the den. Stig joins them together; Barney realises they make a chimney. Shows how the two collaborate and their different cultural backgrounds.

● A steel axe: Barney brings this to the den. Stig appreciates its power and can use it better than Barney, indicating his superior skill in some areas.

● Jelly-babies: offered to Stig and Barney by the Snargets. Stig is, at first, appalled when he sees them being eaten, regarding them as sacred objects.

● Nuts and pistons: Stig takes these from the thieves' car. He uses them to decorate his den, suggesting appreciation of beauty.

● A harp made from a horned animal skull: Stig plays this at the Stone Age camp. He gets carried away by the music, suggesting that even 'in the past' he was creative and something of an outsider.

Teapots, tins and other things

Here are six objects from the story. Who uses them, and how? Why are they important?

Teapot	Tins
A steel axe	Jelly-babies
Nuts and pistons	A harp made from the horned skull of an animal

READ & RESPOND: Activities based on *Stig of the Dump*